From This House to the White House

Rosemary Ferguson Robertson

and

Jennifer Ferguson Peters

Illustrated by Rosemary Ferguson Robertson

A Very Special Thank You to Anne Kearns

Mrs. Kearns,

Thank you for your unyielding dedication to higher education and students of all ages. Thank you for passing on your love of art, homes and interiors for all to appreciate. I learned from you that family and faith should always come first. You have been a great inspiration to me as a working mom.

With love and gratitude,

Rosemary

DEDICATION

With love and gratitude to our family and friends

To Grandma, our "Mom Mom", for raising us to love Scranton and our Irish roots.

To Jenna, Rose, Kate, Gavin and Emily for making everyday a gift. You are our inspiration and the future of Scranton!

There once was a boy whose name was Joe,

who grew up in this house
many years ago.

Now on this street
where he was a resident,
it was named for
George Washington, our
very first President.

Joe loved to play baseball with his friends and always did what was right.

And when he'd climb
the stairs in this house,
he'd say his prayers each night.

Joe loved his friends dearly and they were really quite the bunch. Hank's Hoagies
was where
they would stop,
to always have their lunch.

One day
Joe's dad announced,
he had some news to
share.

It was time for their
family to make a move;
they were heading to
Delaware.

Joe wiped a tear
from his eye and thought,
goodbye for now.

I'll be a true friend to Scranton,
he vowed to
show them somehow.

Joe grew from a child,
and now was a man.
He became a
United   States   Senator
and made a great plan.

From Wilmington
to Dover,
and everywhere
in between,
Delaware was just
wonderful
and everyone agreed.

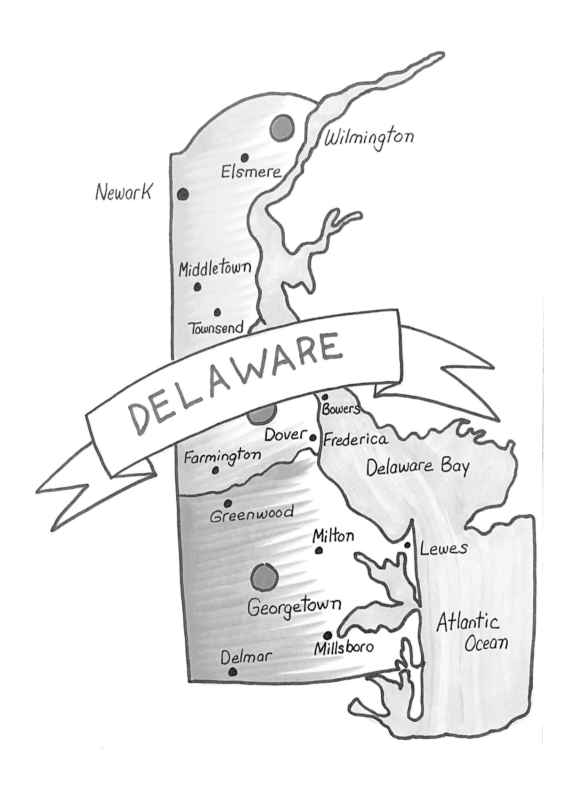

And though Joe
experienced
much heartache
and tears,
with family and friends
beside him, he made it
through the years.

Joe continued
a life of service
to others,
and always remembered
the words of his mother.

Not every day will be great
Mom Mom would explain,
but Joe always persevered
and got on that train.

And because of these words told by his mama, this boy became Vice President for Barack Obama.

This man would not rest until his work was done.

And this boy named
Joe Biden
became our 46th President
in 2021!

This is the childhood home of the 46th President of the United States of America, Joseph R. Biden Jr.

This home is located in the Green Ridge section of Scranton, Pennsylvania.

Today, the street sign near this home has been renamed "Joe Biden Way".

The End

About the Authors

Rosemary Ferguson Robertson and Jennifer Ferguson Peters are sisters and best friends, who were born and raised in the Minooka section of Scranton. They are the daughters of the late Joseph D. and Rosemary Connor Ferguson. They have two brothers Joe, and Tim and wife Julie who also reside in Scranton. They are blessed to be surrounded by an enormous support system of family, friends and neighbors in the city they love, Scranton.

Roe and Jenn are graduates of Marywood University which overlooks the former Biden homestead.

Roe holds a Bachelor of Fine Arts in Interior Design, and a Master of Arts in Art Education from Marywood University. She is an Intermediate School Art Teacher in the Scranton School District and has been teaching for 22 years. Roe feels lucky that her passion and her career are the same thing. When she is not in the classroom, Roe enjoys shopping, with her amazing 15 year old daughter Jenna. Roe and Jenna are inseparable and can often be found performing random acts of kindness. They can also be found painting, drawing or redecorating a room.

Jennifer holds a Bachelor of Science in Nursing from Marywood University and a Master of Science in Nursing from Case Western Reserve University. After a career in nursing in Scranton, Cleveland and New York City, she and her husband Chris returned to the Scranton area to raise their family. Jenn is the proud mom of Rose 15, Kate 13, Gavin 11 and their 1 year old Shih Tzu "Fergie". Jenn enjoys everything her kids are doing including sports and school activities. Jenn is currently a stay at home mom who also enjoys spending time outdoors, decorating and weekend gatherings with family and friends.

Made in the USA
Thornton, CO
07/20/23 20:34:27

044833f1-0a61-4e10-8485-4486c98b9631R01